The Bug Watch

by Cass Hollander

illustrated by Becky Allen James

MODERN CURRICULUM PRESS

Pearson Learning Group

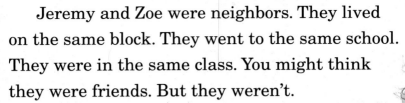

Jeremy and Zoe were neighbors. They lived on the same block. They went to the same school. They were in the same class. You might think they were friends. But they weren't.

Jeremy liked playing soccer and hanging out with his best friend, Chip. He didn't especially like Zoe.

Zoe liked playing the violin and hanging out with her best friend, Claire. She didn't especially like Jeremy.

3

At school, their class was working on a nature project. They called it "Bug Watch." Every day they went out to a field near school to see bugs. When they saw a bug, they would look it up in a bug book. They would find out its name, and write it in a notebook.

Their teacher, Mr. Webb, said that most of the animals in the world were insects. He said you could get an idea of how many bugs there were by sitting in one spot and just looking.

So that's what the class was doing. They'd been venturing outside each day for a week. So far they had identified twenty-seven different bugs.

On Bug Watch, everyone worked with a partner. Chip was always Jeremy's partner. Claire was always Zoe's. But on one occasion, Chip and Claire were both absent. Jeremy and Zoe had to work together.

They sat quietly on a rock. They heard a melody of buggy sounds.

"Be careful, Zoe," teased Jeremy. "There are probably snakes in the grass."

Zoe ignored him. She was scared of snakes. But she wasn't going to let Jeremy know that.

Jeremy picked up a stick and rustled the grass. No snakes slithered around. Instead a grasshopper jumped out. Zoe looked it up in the bug book. Then she furiously wrote "long-horned grasshopper" in her notebook.

They also saw a ladybug, two white
butterflies, a bumblebee, and four ants.

Suddenly, they heard a chirp. Then they
heard another chirp.

"That's a cricket," said Jeremy. "Write
that down."

"But we just heard it chirp. We haven't seen
it," said Zoe. "We don't know what kind of cricket
it is."

Jeremy looked in the bug book. "Well, we're
in a field," said Jeremy. "So, it's probably a field
cricket. Write that down."

"Not until we see it," said Zoe, peering at the ground. She heard another chirp. She pushed apart the grass and saw a thin brown insect about an inch long. "There it is," she said.

"As I said," said Jeremy, "it's a field cricket."

Zoe ignored him. "Do you have a little box?"

"A box?" asked Jeremy.

"Never mind," said Zoe. She reached in her pocket and pulled out a small box that she had been using to hold an eraser and some paperclips.

"Hold out your hand," she told Jeremy.

He did. Then she dumped the eraser and paperclips into his hand.

"What are you doing?" asked Jeremy.

"I'm going to adopt this cricket," said Zoe. "It will be my pet."

"Who ever heard of a bug for a pet?" asked Jeremy.

Mr. Webb had. He thought adopting a cricket was a great idea. He helped Zoe make a cage for the cricket out of some berry baskets. He asked Zoe to keep the class posted on the pet cricket. He suggested that Jeremy visit the cricket at Zoe's house.

"Fat chance that I'll be venturing over there!" said Jeremy.

Every day, Mr. Webb asked Zoe about her cricket, and every day, Zoe had something to tell. She told about the melody the cricket sang. She told how the cricket liked cucumber slices.

When she claimed that the cricket recognized her voice, Jeremy had heard enough.

"A bug can't do that!" said Jeremy furiously.

"It can," said Zoe.

"Jeremy," said Mr. Webb, "since you question it, you should go to Zoe's house and find out for yourself."

So, after school, Jeremy went home with Zoe to see the cricket.

The cricket was in its little cage on the back porch. Everything was quiet. The cricket wasn't making a sound. But as soon as Zoe said, "Cricket, I'm home," it started to chirp.

"See?" smiled Zoe.

Jeremy had to admit it. As soon as Zoe talked, the cricket had begun to chirp.

Jeremy looked at the cricket and at Zoe.

"Not bad!" he said. "Maybe we can be partners again sometime."

"Sure," said Zoe. "How about tomorrow? It will be a special occasion. I'm going to let the cricket go free at the next Bug Watch. He just asked me to."

Jeremy looked at Zoe, amazed.

"Really?" he asked.

Zoe just smiled.